The Manchester Bee

a story about love and hope

Peter A. Johnson

If you enjoy the book then please do leave a review!

Reviews are really important as they help other readers find out more about the book. The more readers there are, the more people the story will reach.

Also author of
'Bog…The Ogre In The Cellar'

Buy it now on
amazon

Why not visit his website

www.peterajohnsonbooks.com

and download some free character sketches from the book for your kids to colour in!

You can follow the author on social media using the handle **@pajthewriter** on all of the platforms below.

ISBN: 978-1-8384211-1-3

This book is dedicated to the city that swarmed together in its hour of need.

The day started well,
There was a buzz in the air,

Impressive, loving, honest and real,
The Manchester bee doesn't lose its appeal.
A flap of its wings,

A dash and a dive,
In between the bricks,
Into the sky.

There is something special in this old town.
From Piccadilly Gardens to Ancoats, we're proud.
Folk are so busy but we still stop to chat
The Manchester Bee rests upon someone's hat!

It's nice to be nice, up north, it's what we do,

A culture so rare it's like you're at the zo

A zoo full of creatures,

The bee's buzzin' sound,

Rests upon an apple,

That it's just found.

It takes it in,

The ups and the downs,

It flies up high,
To the rain and then the sun,
Looks down upon the city,
Which it calls its home.

A home it loves,
The place it lives,
When you think you've had enough,
The more it gives.

A community moving all by themselves,
The key workers busy stocking the shelves.

They're what we need,

They keep us alive,

Whilst the bee

is busy building its hive.

Again we smile; it's what we do
We act with kindness through and through,
A patch of land to have a rest.
Beside the stones and the roses feeling blessed

A little oasis,
Underneath the sky,
That sometimes has clouds,
It's the sparkle in my eye.

It lands upon a bench
to make someone smile
The old lady sits
and watches awhile.

But she's not scared,
Joy fills her heart,
Never does love
tear her apart.

The town folk are gently
moving around,
The pitter-patter of feet
across the ground
The bee was there when
we all felt down,

There by our side,
Buzzing loud,
I'll remember that
till my dying day,
Never forget the Mancunian Way.

The Royal Theatre with Laughter and Love. The Manchester Bee flies above.

Nothing but kindness
no bit of malice,
the bee pops by to Affleck's Palace.

We remember everything,
All of the times,
When the mills popped up and
we worked the mine,

The bee was there then,

then,

It kept us safe,

Safe with each other,

It made us brave.

Off it flies to wander around,
See children playing
the other side of town.
They swing on swings,
They kick their balls,

The bee collects pollen,
To take back home,
It visits the flowers,
Sits on a gnome.

People gather,
Tell jokes that are funny,
But the bee keeps working,
To make its honey.

And at the end of each day,
as the sun goes down,
The bee sits
quietly feeling proud,
Proud of its home,
And everything within it,
The Manchester Bee has no limits